The Depth of Existence

by

Rebecca Mummery

Published by New Generation Publishing in 2013

Copyright © Rebecca Mummery 2013

First Edition

The author asserts the moral right under the Copyright, Designs and Patents Act 1988 to be identified as the author of this work.

All Rights reserved. No part of this publication may be reproduced, stored in a retrieval system or transmitted, in any form or by any means without the prior consent of the author, nor be otherwise circulated in any form of binding or cover other than that which it is published and without a similar condition being imposed on the subsequent purchaser.

www.newgeneration-publishing.com

 New Generation **Publishing**

A Return To Solitary Party
(Bereft of Faith)

Galloping at the sunset like wild horses,
peering strenuously at distance,
face to face with a million miles unreachable;
the seas stood between, so low with sin, lust;
lust in a million creases of aged essence;
Sea – an essence of my abundant wishes.
to become engulfed in the sunset,
once young and seeking trouble now
old in head, all infant troubles between I and
vermillion arched fire that many yearn to see.

My eyes grew out of my head at my feet,
through planted seeds I took from my heart.
Sometimes, I am overwhelmed by temptation to kick it,
and watch it roll like an unloved stone, away; be gone
God's art.
Frustrated like the deaf; all touch like the blind,
watch the ball of confusion from the highest abode.
The air does not ail pink corners of the earth of my
sight,
instead a dress washed upon the shore; scrambled like
stranded to meet my vigil I had so long kept alive with
the seas, but I could not fit into it.
Old in head, I held no faith to dress for occasion when I
was with
face pressed up to the sunset, to oblivion,
alas, when night hung over the world of Reverend.
Doom's surplice,
I put on the dress.
I hoped at best I would abandon, align my sights, step
fervently

with conscience, away from some family of water,
but when I returned to the party,
Everyone had left.
It is through faith I let drown,
through the surrendering of my sights,
my loved ones.
The angels, in light dressing gowns,
did not stay for me, because of my fights,
I gave them up like the faith.
But I'm sure a lesson learnt,
they'll come around again,
for the delightful, beautiful cycle,
the race for the created never ends
and bend my ear to the highest,
power that looms Godley over my bed...

Wherever that may be...

Cavalier of Sorry Portents

Drunken admirers who brushed past her curves –
they were only sweeping through her like birds...

But every day a different gentleman brushed past her
like nothing before – no bird, it was a wave imported
from the strongest ocean;
slow, slow, he turned.

They wore black, they always made sure:
*"If you can find light in me, then it will show
when we exchange a look..."*

Shallow, the perverted, they know how to prey –
they held only weighty ego afoot their lightest gate...

But another gentleman sometimes rested a weighty set
of fingers upon his gate, so heavy.
Like the conscience of crime,
wide open or not at all; perchance in consequence there
shall be no love
and oh so wide of its skies.

They wore black, they always made sure:
*"If you can find light in me, then it will show
if my eyes cannot follow your own, when they tear and
barely open..."*

Even those who made move in kindness –
they were only stirring themselves; once a stationary
sky at best.

But another gentleman was constantly approaching her
like no other mortal could do – his manner of

progression was thunder
from more than a sky.
The universe of unearthly constellations that doth not
spare thee:
pulsing, contracting, expanding, and chanting their
spontaneity –
he was neither fleeting nor blatantly sunk into his body,
stationary.

They wore black,they always made sure:
"If you can find light in me, then it will show
when you fall in love, blinded by its power to guide
you..."

But the lady had completed the gallery of portraits in
motion,
for numerous days; fluctuating fantasies like dripping
lotion.
And they repeat, abstract notion from his eye,
became so much a wealth of sense to someone so shy.
But he stays young, and terminally all for her,
the love equilibrium – a balance of the reject and insert
button,
the cat will bite before it purrs,
but protective all the same, whatever its feeling
adapting to situation
after another.
And one man's reclamation
in the timid, flamboyant lady:
"I can recover your heart, if only you let me"...
"No", she cried: "I'd rather it done with..."
And she, like the buried, had no more to give,
but the man cried forth and peeled back the door on its
heel;
there stood a priest in emerald garment,
a frown of disdain, and no more portraits in that

loveable gallery to see!

Charlatan Cannibals

The creed of my belief,
fluttered about my room; injured wings
Et Cetera. The floor beneath
full of rejoicing folk in spiritual fashion
who wore rings.

Perseverance constructed my key,
before the spiritualists kept me alert.
Alert – I passionately disagreed,
with their perennial, evergreen tree;
Its progression from fraudulent birth,
which apparently grew out of God's placid earth,
but I believe it grew out of me...

But my floundering, feeble article,
doth wore the headline: "Smile";
for half my raging bull
stripped a charlatan of his pride.

At times, my chasten torture
is clad in treasured bones,
albeit, no nutrient is half, nor quarter kosher,
on tongue made of common copper, not gold!

To You, Ana

A friend stitched my passion,
it's formerly what I expected.
Permanence, an infected prayer,
both my palms met for a heart,
and had made ideals
I was intent on catching,
belong to merciless, driving
blood of untrue companies
from long ago,
somewhere.

However, mended passion of my own,
took and drew those hands out
from beneath the bodily armour,
that concealed strength undetermined.
And you eyed my solitaire from the
rust of the courageous element
to the relief of a wealth of gold,
because in every room of the world,
I lie upon a chaise cloud to let open
my thoughts to the muse of our
friendship,
of which, like the emotion-twirling
drum of drama has temperament,
my reverie is not idle with a driving
of no other passengers but I,
and now I am truly alive with
a stranger Devil
free.

Winter in various apparels of shades
of perishing the visage,
I thought it mine and thoroughly

thought another permanence so
beyond the pale, towards the
curtain slithering rough across its rail;
just the final wait to become bereft
of at least one permanent reason to live
and lie in all rooms upon planks of
wood, disheartened.
But your fresh carination of the one
constellation
to give me all other seasons,
hooked through my prayer and I
was temporarily curious with caution
of what had flown away.
But of now, I am like the bird of prey,
I am destined
to embrace our kindred way and life
itself because we are mostly the same,
mortar to make assembly of the
wishes so strong.
We live in peace in the home they
call companionship,
despite the wolf that blows west wind,
eternity has life and death so long.

The Wish

If my wish to a deafened deity,
you would merely stand at the wall.
Alas, a thousand claret brushes
you paint me,
stirring, curling, luring
my heart of gold,
out of the abysmal darkness
of a hole.

We love at clarity – destroying
distance,
and your backbone crumbling
so slowly,
when your hands are employing
polished bricks for a business,
intoxicated, under the whiskey seas
that gives carination to that
brute of so little time
that stole thee!

But what looms devote in the
higher, incredible kingdom,
is not consistence of curse –
my wish for you, my love,
is an anchor of those signalling
bells you hear…

So ring them…

Sacrifice for your pleasure,
separated from the agony –
I am a first, away from love,
driven in a whore's polished hearse!

The Time and Man

Time was beneath and over his head,
as every valley was one bright in transit,
and sore snake skin he shed,
bright, young, swirling debris.
Why such a sky so full of red,
eternally young from what she bred,
…why a time before, every valleys'
throbbing heart so primitive, so candid?

To his wonder he was within a valley
like any other depressed to the stone,
redressed his head with thorns,
not so sad to see (so dressed alone),
as when the skies would become apparent
and beat, the catastrophe that they too live –
he postponed,
eternally, and some desire that cracked
virtue, cracked his skull and he found
two tones,
…why is there no river after every sea, he
cried until sore…

But he bled because he made it possible,
the skies no longer felt,
stream valley so bright as whatever
as may be seen in Heaven,
time, you take no prisoner out of the deep,
he would later weep.
And time replied as dry as the dead, old skies…
madness you designed my hands
to take yourself apart in greed unholy,
those trees, the pillars of your desire,
…still stand,

Alas! I will stare them to depression,
he spoke so slowly…

Grey is a figment too fair,
to pepper the time these days.

Compensation

He is wondrous as the rarity,
of a rainbow relished by my eye,
serenely staining for a short while
its territory,
I cannot make an aftermath of
oblivion,
in the head where a sweet
martyr had died.

Because your pain, I pondered,
made destruction of a drought,
Alas!
not too much compensation
complimentary to compassion, of
which effortlessly wandered
and,
so not a martyr of now.

I would give you my last breath
my love, in an everlasting cycle,
for the world itself is round...

Beast Without Paradise

He was neither proud nor holding his hand
against a reflection of Guilt with upturned lips,
young perfumes from aged necks were all around,
closing on the twenty-something fire and running
its course
of his juvenile desires, eclipsed.

Young hands were sweeping the wood on which
he rested deeply in love with the grasp
of Eurydice,
but she was cold, old and deeply amiss
in his world he contrived from her eye and
gave kiss, to give past a paradise.

And may he scrunch in his power,
veined-eyelids in nightmares
that run after,
his charm within the beast he is
characteristic of a man in Paris plaster,
slip, slip,
away with the masquerade of age
and he tears his face off with unbelievable
courage,
but made one of unbridled youth that would
not grow,
flourish…

Drowning (by the beach)

In the theatre of fever on faces,
their fashion is a myriad of fret,
I laughed from the tier, closed curtain,
silhouette of fear, open wide, allow
but not just yet.
The trees of madness waving arms,
plea for reality I could not give them
their faces back for a minute in
which they clambered my tower
and made a falsity of my guard.

Backdrops of sea and I was all
at confusion.
They lay on the sands in pain,
seizure, pleasing my hungry eye
for dying,
and I was living in the seats
with my armour; distorted rest
on my knees of bone,
and I was with the disciples
of Christ in merry old ways
of betraying fortunes,
and betraying ways of life,
I plunged deep…

In my room,
against the backdrop of tarnished-ash
walls,
my back lost its independence
as the pendulum swung
into my grey, narrow eye
of what God gave me,
a sting of regret, he told me,

he beckoned inverted,
he whispered "Good-bye".

Murder, Do Not Please

An ammunition we could not name,
could not take apart,
we could not use it against
another, in kindred form.
What we consider an aim,
the murderer of a palm,
fingers acquaint with a rigid
arrow, propelled and sent like
lightning separate from our storm,
between you and I a distance,
a length the weaponry must
walk; wander wide, to rid us,
of a somewhat heavier alter.
He was adorned in its own silk,
that rushed down his body,
find, have found and do not falter,
his eyes were fully bred
from romance, and full of milk.

Ammunition, it could never be used
against, only for, for you.
Love dismantled and to wound you
partially, not properly would be
considered irreparable, immutable,
indeed.
Palms of lines, it's merely a pattern
I find, nor strings of age to murder,
nor rivers of deceit to only please.

Aegri Somnia

A sick man's dreams,
he cannot live them during
sleep's coma,
though when awake in the
spotlight, filtered through the
blinds- the Sun beams
and despite its visit not
making on the walls of eternal
duration,
some positive, everlasting mural,
the spotlight evokes a
sick man's dream from
conscious thought, the moment…

When he does not believe
he is sick.

Cognitive Staircase, Red

My love felt like a pain in the head,
immunity, tragedy and a heart like thunder.
My love for him like a thorn in the side,
some heart is only half dead,
half the love cut from my red soul, under,
stepped like something fragile, outside,
to find him beneath God, beneath the starry life
of the cemented partnership of souls,
that had me dwelling the blues,
dwelling up the cognitive staircase of garment scarlet.
Bleed my half-lovesick soul,
for the love of a man, who wore the carpet like a cloak,
he cloaks the night in a heartfelt rainbow,
of hot suns and vermillion empowerment,
towards my heart, towards my enigmatic eye.
He powerfully came on foot, and a tiptoe,
such a subtle look my way, the lapidary monument
of gesture,
my eye turned a stone age grey.
Well, every examination of his demeanour –
I saw raw familiarity, saw myself
in his way,
I could ask to give him all my affection,
Alas, I predict, I say,
I will only turn a shade greener,
When he leads me backwards down a bled staircase,
When he leads me home to the size of true heart,
When I am smaller; misplaced power,
into his playful eyes.
He takes me forward; he takes me back,
through huddling masses of mare in sluttish lace,
perchance, he reckons me a mare,
Reckons me without morals,

Reckons my sweetness is merely tasting of sour,
When I beckon him my love in code.
And that such a scarlet heart must be bleeding black,
That my intentions dark,
That my land is grass,
always growing, always thrusting through the
resistance of cruel air,
his rejection; the coolest air I have ever felt,
but I feel whatever he feels to rest my head,
upon my love, my love, my love,
he murdered the bark.
Now I see, it must have been delusion,
I see gentlemen, I see sex, and I am lust,
Alas, every tree that I have seen,
does not, cannot thrust through the gates of my love,
my love,
compare, do you dare?
I will reject like he rejected me,
the cool air on my shoulder,
I give to you,
You feeble skyline blue,
tread upon my staircase,
I will make your lust for me frozen in time,
love has made me colder, thus that marginally older,
pain ages the once spritely youth...

Perchance, he will sleep on garment red...
Atop the staircase – His passions read,
I have grown so ugly in protest
of my violence,
my smaller heart – the main part,
of such decadent romance,
I kicked him to the end,
I kick-started a love lost...

Cygnet Compassion

Young swans are indelible
upon the lake,
in Winter's evening hours
they make
the outline of a fictional
love heart,
because long, slender necks
bend delicately not to make a star.

The lake is made indelible
with rose petals,
The cool Autumnal days
make a thousand golden medals,
transform the place into
the Heavens
because gold is not scattered
lightly, and peppered.

Swans float effortlessly upon
the brocade seas,
made so with cyclamen floating
colours, shrouding the Hades,
swans bow like corn
in Joseph's dreams…

*Compassion for the dead, died in
the lake that keeps
their souls like they keep their
dreams…*

Darkness

Darkness, it's been more than
the duration of Jack the Ripper
found
and I cannot even begin to recall,
your presence is the sound,
of my tongue caught: silence
to breathlessly enthral.

Darkness, it's been more than
immortality's journey to
the unspoken other side
and you with no face – did
you ever foresee,
your darkness to which light,
had you died...?

Sometime
asleep with eyes open,
you will recall me,
before you die too...

Darkness II

Darkness, you threw my
bones to the black dog,
you hauled your arrow
through the apple of my tree,
an equally dangerous game
for which I was the fire
to my logs
and a sight stretched beyond
the window pane, but your
presence enough, ever dreary.

Darkness, my old flame
I held to light my way,
my old flame to enlighten my
dark, old road with lighter tone
of my daily Halloween,
a dangerous game aboard that
ghost train –

The throne endows the young
girl queen,
With the power to perish,
With the power to burn away...

Dear Demigod

Tell me the place to wander,
I demand it from my deity heart,
where I might find, lest I am to squander,
my whole span of existence made of two halves.
Dear demigod, accept your mortality
and deliver me,
I fear another portion of my fruit would
be unbearable,
Deity, we share one fruit – He will do
worse than hate me,
Hell's thunder; Satan's roar from the
mouth-shaped pit of Zeus,

(That's what he can do...)

Dear demigod, the rock is definitely not wearable,
Prometheus may wear it like hard cloth upon his back,
only his magic produced another fruit – a brand of
succulent betrayal both you and I could feed upon.
But temptation will give birth to I again, upon myself
with the pain of consequence!

Many men march deserts,
with specialties of failure from arrogance,
But let me allow ourselves,
to find the place before I die.

We'll make a new world there,
dear demigod, you could save us both!

Dance and Dine

The angels caught me teetering across
vast, black flames with a stranger,
but a stranger; acquainted with frequence,
after many a sequence, like an
animal that knew the way back, the
stranger was as feigned as,
the masquerade of stabs in the black
by contemporary delinquents,
who had recently reared their audacity
and approacheth I with
an infiltration of privacy
and the questions they asked me:

Secrets, identities, and loved ones,
balancing the strings of my heart...

"Did I sever the strings?
Because if I am pulled..." –
I cut through, and my coveted contents
must
be still intact,
as bludgeoned and heavily wounded, my back.

Stranger was he,
met many prior,
but the angels and me
sought clandestine refuge and triumphed
the flames, and held within, those love-lost liars
and in between individual curling, spiralling
single-tone fires,
I took Grandmother's strength of spirit,
let the stranger maintain his sharp, old dance,
I stood in my bedroom, in prudish pivot,

frightened, weary of forming some
devilish, hypnotic steps toward a vigilant pit!

But soon, did I venture,
to a sweet, delight of sparkling smile;
timeless, angelic cadence,
to which I stepped and what grew to form –
To dance from my heart – my penchant,
to be fed from the played-down plate of modesty,
I can dance, and I can dine,
served by the angels, never fatigued, never gaunt,
Grandmother, my angel,
who bestowed in me belief, fuelled by rational honesty.

Deceived By All

They; an unctuously, fire-breathing
assemble,
Burns me too much with
a kind fire – it burns,
Acceptance – it is but urge
as all my gullibility trembles,
I paid for this error,
from potential companionship,
I – severed
and retreat back in the lone wolf
I am always likely to be.

Vernal traps of Spring,
they too are unctuously sneering
As I search for a beautiful something,
during what I can only recall
As a Winter's breathing,
that Spring dressed in hopeful apparel,
But loitering in their breath was
no succession of Christmas carol,
T'was Winter for sure
and looks in the time deceive me.

Denature It

Denature the soul,
worthless now
it's not our own.
Use it for the fireplace,
whenever we run short
on coal,
throw it in,
pulling it out of our chests
like string.
For we have grown
worthless ourselves,
out of shape, out of place,
with skin so thin,
a walking waste.

And denature the ground,
so it will not hold
our weight in pounds.

Denature the water,
worthless now,
the ocean's distant daughter.
Use it to decorate the paths
of our sordid lives,
liquid matter we won't be
able to keep once caught,
Let it sift out of the cracks
in our palms,
and roll down our useless
arms.
For it has become some sort
of vapour,
not a survival to keep us here,

starving, at loss, and all the while
that harmless air remains so calm,
for us it no longer reliably caters.

And denature the wine,
so it will not make of us,
pathetic, self-absorbed mass
of swine through time.

Denature the pen,
worthless now,
scratching at some white,
use it to make our cries for
help.
And when not in black and white,
who knows whether what we've
written is at all right,
or whether it is a farcical affair,
by the dear in distress with the
long flaxen hair.
And no one is to blame but us,
we were not willing to lend,
before we changed our soul
for the worst.
And now everything we hold up
in the skies,
has become our foreground,
driven in that gloomy hearse.

And denature the books,
so that they will turn over themselves,
whenever we try to look.

And denature the Gods,
denature their generosity,
so we will become blasted unto

extinction,
from the world of which we made
of it – *atrocity*.

Former Bachelor

Sat in the silent nights of Africa,
pondered did I,
of how I may trace a former bachelor,
yes, famous – he may lie,
into my telescopic eye,
upon the other hand, he may deny,
such elegantly pressed fingerprints
on his love-fuelled thighs.

Extravagance arose without grace,
other times t'was anchored underground,
like the blind man's sight caught face,
a voice of Racism was caught
and found dead in one morality crowd.

There exists no pearly grey matter,
in between black and white logic of the pessimist.
No rings barricading the skull of Saturn,
when I pressed against once bachelor, a kiss.

Actions speak more volume than words,
in the silent nights of Africa,
for I built up my yearning here,
to make love to a former bachelor.

Dolls

Rouge tinted faces;
a production line
of dolls,
in the shining light
of Sol.

Guardian Angel

He is my guardian angel,
shakes me kindly with asperity,
rocks my wooden manger,
locks me out of my Depression territory.

He grasped roughly my upper arm,
I felt arousal, but more so affection;
disarmed of my ruthless palm
doth creased, clasping Devil's messenger.

My desire for the angel is immutable;
he, clad in dark shades of the night,
the emergence of his night eyes is crucial,
because without – no contagious sight.

He once caught a glimpse of Heaven,
I catch it every time,
in day, in night, I rise level,
to meet his healing eyes...

My Guardian Angel,
stripped of the armour he wore for me,
Adonis! Adonis! His godly body!
...the ultimate sex I see.

Heart of Infinity

Up the hill of true love
we clambered,
naked as birth we were,
our hands knotted
against an air so candid,
aged and full of cure.
Not a drop of life's elixir,
because we thus born,
were neither standing
nor laid frozen waiting, for
the wild wonder of
immortality.

We leapt into each other's
bones,
clinging softly for the
asperities of romance,
into a life succeeding
this, as barely souls.
But a bowman's dance,
thus great time we hesitantly
cowered and crouched,
in actual fact not perishing,
we were pacing
toward the heart of infinity.

We did not take
advantage of tongue to
survive spoken –
the sensation of touch
had already opened
its mouth,
and Cupid's bow danced

its way jet straight;
meant some fantastic
fantasy – not about.
And Cupid narrated
so much of how to one another
we doused,
an animal afraid of its
prey its cool Summer rain,
its will to kill; for
confronted with
reflection we regain
normality we have
always had to
cradle above our heads –
the halo self-assembled
for complete control of
our kindness.

We remained so kind,
when low in circumstance
of the time, it is tyrant we find
lightly pressed to the worsened infants,
for they grow to a height above their parents,
grow distraught leaving some park brothel.
But we, progressing the race with both feet
and flight with bare foot pounding the ground
trying to split the flyer of purity,
and eventually doing so with passion full,
and fiery souls within that cool,
experienced world.
So kind we were, crouched, crying,
that tyrant made us weep,
but we turned that flyer into
a cloth to clothe us, of Love,
but upon the hill,
we did not need it anymore,

Needed not that evidence to the eye.
We were laughing and could not stifle,
laughter caught by the winds,
winds blew it about and life pulled a rifle
on our minds' carefully crafted strings,
but the strings of our shared, large heart are pinned,
to the skies, and God plays them like a
beautiful harp of gold.
For we controlled our love of kindness in
our flamboyant days like a playing musician,
but of now – God, a musician, controls
our Love with not kindness, but without any intention,
because our Love, a flourished flower,
an immortality, that is not questioned,
not made up to become,
unlike the morphing of bodies through period,
from birth we were the fullest of hearts,
Bowman's arrow amongst the blood from passage,
our mothers conceived in strength
the hill of future,
us babies at present, the sacrament,
glitter love-stained eyes,
and the rest was raring for the hill.
Then eyes were closed,
the glitter died,
then reopened a top the hill...

I saw no sight truer than a landscape of red,
the world of the town, of the birthplace,
under a veil of our tarnished flyer,
we sought escapism of their world so dire.

I heard no sound truer than his hungry breath,
heard no breath with the conviction.
Convicted men dragged in manacles, with passionate
weep,

he wept through eyes of the gentle sky,
a hill that midway, he thought was too steep,
in the end proved a lie.

I tasted no flavour truer than the flavour perched flatly upon his marinated lips,
like one feather of the bird's plumage upon a chapped old branch.
Branch reunited with what made the bird fly away,
bird shot by a dancing bowman,
I killed an aging boy,
his wing resting on the branch.
It blew away...

We all deserve that chance again,
young boy's gruesome chance to be alone.
He deserved solitude that flew away so suddenly from Love,
I aimed point blank,
my love's jagged body sank,
and in anxiety, I shrank...
If he stood back up, like the immunity of new soul,
I had found my love at long last
and he arose, touching the branch as he grew unbeaten,
the feather flew
and then I knew,
I was confronted with something I had never seen face
and I confess, I felt no sensation truer,
than our Love...

I, the bowman,
I, the bowman
and we danced upon the hill,
danced, ascending toward another world,
Toward another realm,
Toward the heart of infinity...

His Midnight Eye

He had lost that glimmering
crescent of his eye,
the colour dimmer in
his midnight eye,
o' vigilant sage of nocturne
in the pupil of his eye,
how his mind taught
it thorough
the observation that must gather
in his midnight eye.
All senses; touch, smell, an ear
will abidingly and electronically
cover, for
what is the
sight and his identical brother,
lips will shrivel,
and utter not a word,
nostrils will stay un-phased,
fingers will dither
on in lazy malaise
cracking – showing
its anger days,
and all the while,
pictures will slither,
into that midnight eye.
The heavily populated world,
in his midnight eye.

His Ruby Heart

There are times in the shining
light of Sol
that I, beneath reflective panes,
am silently pining
for a certain man's baritone
and the bait to maul
in this spritely hall,
where my heart is shining
like ruby jewel the size of fist.
My once textured heart
now a bloody stone,
absence is an art,
for when toward materialistic
pleasures, we can never resist
and for all absence is
paining at the start...
To gently bleed the stone hard heart.
And inside the dreams,
release my phantom pain through
punch and hiss!
That woman – a tart
is approaching in manner of flirtation –
my Prince!

...although it is beginning to seem...
he too, a thousand deserts apart...
truly has as I
a Ruby Heart.

Infatuation Vanity Affair

Yonder upon the shattered
portrait in motion,
it moves as I wish,
its life-long promotion,
reflecting of me
something garish!

Its frontier of darkened
steel,
I, estranged inside,
but the mirror does not
feel
the essence of me that
died!

Scattered upon the floor
of carpet black,
frozen fish still, in
the oil-polluted sea.
Silvery transparency
I so lack,
when it does not reflect
of me!

Peroration with this
shattered mirage,
A mirror copying my
faces' cracks,
A broken, petty visage,
though it means the world
to purified glass!

The glass and I –

we are united,
A couple of solitudes
occupying one space,
A single solitude sighted,
in my reflected,
pernicious face!

A mockery of one
every night and day,
Every time I occupy
the sheltered life,
Every time I try to play
life's pernicious rules,
for all I am, a shattered
housewife!

It Was Home

Moss stalks up lapidary brick
like clematis
climbing toward the Heavens
with colourful offering,
though this growth is a
dirty green,
telling of tenants lives in
the gutter.
Cenotaph drainpipes,
cerise lips crying
at the drainpipes,
derived from the eye's watering waste.
Water the flower lips
with salt tears,
to spurn sorrow's growth,
and sadness laughter,
beneath this colossal canopy,
a derelict construction,
what once was home,
bereft of life,
bereft of families' fruit,
once ready and ripe,
ready to be taken,
in what once was such a
home grown life,
and rest my own weary bones,
beside the bones of my wife,
whilst the cold contaminates the air.
And it cuts through the living
like some carving knife,
This is life,
This is life.

Lady Lazarus

How mauled some lady lies,
bitten big and generously.
Her muse of worship –
shall he let her, Lady Lazarus, be,
and drag her back through her
shallow grave
to restore the life he took, her
peril, his nature of a fiend!

Author's Note:
I did not realise the title of this poem was also a title of another poem, as I found out after I had written it.

Let it Commence

We can make a war this morning,
we can carry it on to evening late
and war we are always born in,
when we are thrown into the narrow and straight.
Because of this, we indulge in protest,
war is always there
and life is obviously no test,
when it is morally right and fair.
And we can make some peace for now,
but we cannot carry it forward,
we make a class of children bow
to teachers – but this is no good,
children are soldiers from onset
and peace will turn to war,
we are good in where there is debt,
and will act out peace no more.
There will be nothing left,
supple skin left rough and sore
and maybe some good will be kept,
But we will use it all for war.

Lake of Avalon

Hello Love, my heart continues to break,
Love, I need it mended, need it from gravel strong,
back to a fleshy, pumping scarlet lake,
where beneath, the spirit of Avalon,
will forever swim its memorable way,
inside its court of magical romances.
My heart's a growing Camelot, red,
where the chieftain dreamily dances,
so, hello Love, you said like a chieftain
I would lead beyond exploitation of my body,
And so I forgot to forget...

Hello love, my heart has endured many tests of time,
and the young men keep swinging like swaying secrets of sentiment.
Love, cast a spell in the direction of the lively secrets' that bide,
my inevitable bad fortune in the cupped hands of fabricated tenderness.

Hello Love, my heart hit the glass floor
like the plummeting testament out of the hand of atheism,
that meets the floorboard in the home of the Lord
and so, vanity made contact with purity in an act of splintered heart favouritism.

Hello Love, my heart, a youthful Camelot, growing,
no man ever made my heart take flight –
My heart has began ascending; a thin river flowing,
alas, all my muscles of carination giving way to *his* slights...

Hello Love, my Camelot likened to the parked vehicle,
oh no, its vulnerability for no intention marked it
parked,
merely halted in its tracks of what is theoretical,
My theory underneath the wheels,
My theory a habitant under the Avalon Lake in a car.

*Hello Love, my lake of Avalon a reservoir of
squandered blood,
donating blood of my love for him...*

Loose Leant Love Lord

I dreamt of the loose leant Love
Lord,
infused many a man with a weeping
woman,

She wept no more...

He clouded, took away my peripheral
vision, too,
No memory of back,
No notion of forward,
but all life is so accurately mapped
upon and around her
tailored tissue,
because in my loving dream,
I saw he, the devote centaur,
a venturing marriage about
the subtly, soothing paradises,

She was soothed...

And when I awoke so sudden,
the bare, bone trees,
had sloped down to the famous floor,
of which no centaur stood,
but of my mirror mentor –
mentors always failed,
but my mirror, it never spoke,
and my life of love develops like
the serenity held in the reality
of the skies,
no stage – it simply is,
but unseen platforms of mine...

*They are hard to share,
I am hard to give...*

Masochist's Second Chance

He marched into battle, past a pane of glass,
t'was then my heart sank, bypassing its ribbed cage chamber,
how beautiful a man could slowly and steadily gallivant,
into the disgusting common brawl haven?

One bloody-cherry tear,
and the man who could not contain his ugliness would fear,
one woman's cherry-verbal wrath!

I wanted no graze upon his back,
built like the Berlin Wall,
nor bruise; it is stern hard fact
that there are many ways in which a man could fall...

One bloody-cherry droplet,
and I would have removed it in grace,
my rosy lips, cherry from bare, flushed goblet,
and I would have set a new mark upon his face.

Violence can be loving,
we inflict pain upon those we love,
fight fire with fire, because the ruthless buffet,
of venom doth stick a cocktail stick in my mouth,
not of venom, the masochist
craves that bittersweet Love!

Lullaby of Love

At home, a stately citizen,
at best, she is one apart
from destinations too dull –
too satisfying to a slumber heart.
Alas, she is duly bitten
by such bite; it doth literally null,
the array of humane emotion,
excluding the discomfort of sickness.
He always knowingly serves her the Love potion,
and inside of her timeless skull,
a mind doth shiver,
an order from brain,
that lips should quiver,
that perchance, all kinds of eyes must be some river –
For a river lets go,
all of her eyes off show,
though she has yet to know,
if upon waiting, she'll be terminally alone,
or that maybe he will be with her.

Upon waiting, to sleep her heart,
he prepared her for a lock of lips,
equality to which she took the heaviest sips.
A person once more,
but then she saw,
A man asleep,
at her feet, in the dark.

Masters of Ceremony

Through the hue and cry
Of Euthanasia,
Through the sharpness
Of that colossal razor,
Through the predator's pounce,
Of the malkin,
Through that alley
Of conditions dank and dim,
Through the masks
Of Plaster Paris, ashen,
Through the augury
Of the assassin.

Through all such events
Of what is infinitely bad,
The gift is in the right to die,
When eyes and the
Times cry.
The gift is in the harm,
When our existence is carved,
The gift is in the hunting pet,
A token gesture of its debt,
The gift is in the places of damp,
Where there is rejuvenation
Waiting for man,
The gift is in the colour that
Drains and dies,
By no means "pale" in
Rembrandt eyes,
And the gift is in the omen,
For if not, the preparation
Lays dormant.

Of those properties six,
For if we had the audacity
To mix;
And so, through the sharpness
Of the assassin,
All of our worlds would
Plummet, crashing,
Endless Terror!

We are all Masters of Ceremony.

No Man Compares

I took my vacation abroad,
the last I fell into his eyes,
It would have been suffice to prick skin with sword,
from its blunt, old, harmless sides.

My hands would have withdrawn from the frontline,
if I felt them feeling him,
if thumb and forefinger so suddenly began to pluck fine,
toward mine breath of lust his chin.

"Put a restraining order upon me",
I uttered into the ear of my soul,
but in Africa, in distress, I cannot see
nor feel a presence to hold.

Opportunities arise
like the gradual growth of nature,
through the myriad of sexual eyes,
merely sculpt upon aged moon, another crater.

I did not realise,
his essence in men's' disguise,
my sword; his hand as guide,
the only man whom held blood in palm lines.

My Descent into Hell

I
Stood in light's absence,
I prized open the ancient
pocket watch
and the exact present was
not captured,
all sense of time had been
shot,
into the hot sun of oblivion,
and I was at once fearful,
this atmosphere so evil
as the Pharaoh that kills
every boy young
and this destitution of my
soul,
nearing full
of Satan's anguish orchestra,
the screaming violins of
murder
and Jezebel, I swore I heard
her,
I began to demonstrate sins,
I felt them inside of myself,
like a wet needle scraping my
inner being,
And I endured all of this by
myself,
And of only a pitch blackness
I was seeing.

II
I became the time
and decided that it was fair,

that I waded through sprawled
out barks on my level,
but in darkness like this, there
was no shine,
to turn a jewel,
and discover it was simply dark
purple.
And my tousled, hanging hair
resembled that of my soul in
strips,
a wind so dominating,
it blew them about so forcefully
and inserted through the voids
in my lips,
to make of me anti-life,
in a place that was not
accommodating.
And I cannot find that path
of light,
made so by sprinkling of
rays,
the dark cradled in my sight,
with a touch of darkest grey.

III
Oh, it felt like years,
isolated in deepest fear,
Oh, I fear for my life,
its pleas that none will hear,
The distance so far,
too far to reach a single ear,
and so sudden, the ground
became fire.
Did I pass for a cursed one?
Did acceptance into Hell
take years?

Has a life before this
expired?
Has Hell, for me, begun?
But I plead, I did not consent,
to this bleakest of all places
and now emerging faces,
from out beneath the spaces,
All heavy skin, and bone
structures,
All features painfully thin,
is this the place for us,
when we are all guilt-ridden
with Sin.
And I dread to think,
though I am on the brink,
of becoming just like them.

IV
They did not speak to me,
all I heard was sighs,
under the auspices of
that man with horns,
who destroyed what I knew
of the skies
and made of me austere born,
for I was afraid to step some
steps further,
toward the deadened end.
And I, built up with fervour,
In this hellish, demon of events,
sought a place by the fire,
but the closest I could get,
was to stand on this woodland
vast funeral pyre,
where flames did not leave
burning scars,

did not brand me a burned
victim of heat,
But of my soul, it did mar
and of life, I was obsolete.
My God, where is the line,
to cross with huge relief,
Where is the soul of mine
to protect and rightfully keep?
No, what once was my own,
has become the Devil's gift,
from my God I am disowned
and such heavy soul that
no faith can lift.

V
I took role in such hideous play,
directed by the blistered hand,
made so with the sin of jealousy,
cast off from God's own land.
But here, I am to stay,
for he will not turn face away,
From my piteous state,
I am part of his hideous ways,
I admit, I committed heresy,
in God's sharpest eye,
for I named myself a God,
and a disgusting being I died,
only to fall from earth,
and land unto the care of evil,
In abundance, he'll cast his iron,
over my weeping brow,
like Saul who was fed to
lions.
And the difference to consider,
that God had saved him, and
how,

I have no one to save me here,
and alone, I mutter and shiver,
And I am resigned to this for now
and forever,
And when the earth shall shatter
into a trillion pieces,
well, it will not matter,
my agony will not cease,
I damned here for eternity long,
and instruments of that thing
pain,
will drone on in pitiful song,
and never will it stop,
It will carry on,
thereafter and forever more.

VI
A place in Hell does not teach
me,
nor does it preach,
those words of God,
to live by and to keep,
and here in my descent's
garden,
I frown and weep,
and nothing can assuage
the pain and grief
and I am no longer ardent
for the life I carry.
I am a slave to the cardinal
of horror and sorrow
and I have been married
to the day of which none more
shall follow,
This everlasting dirge of a day
in eternal regret,

no happiness or outlet,
to fill what is hollow,
And what is hollow,
is my body and mind,
And of the life I once knew
it is for that I crave and pine,
And now I shall seek a place
to lie,
And at every second, I
shall perish and die,
In the eyes of Satan,
oh, it's approaching late,
and I'm leaping into the
fiery sky below my feet,
my world has been turned
upside down,
And there is no solace,
nor hope for me now.

Oh, Sharp Memory!

Old side streets glitter with menacing past memory
like sky's gentle stars,
Though no gentle impression creeps upon mind and
shoulders,
and recollections make stone of heart,
Tars it lapidary, make full fit the side streets; a
recurrent,
sharpened cemetery...

Does not glaze with softness, one's barely opened
saddened,
glassy eye,
And nothing inside that cosmos or mine will hone one's
eyes like the disguise
Sky has behind the softest breadth of cirrus; those
candid
side streets; fiercely sharp as the sky is maddened...

By the brightness of the fierce Sun that controls the
days
of our lives like hearts control our destinies,
For memory makes sharp, cold bitterness of
despairingly
lenient softness, oh where art thou terrestrial
Entities to build my cosmos; that June or May's mark
one
year before would not be set in its awful ways?

That old side streets would not glitter at all of past
like the fiercely, irreversible Sun's light
Upon a crescent shape half-bitten by its own jealousy –
that it makes glitter of the night when Sun dies,
Spites itself on numerous ends of Day, when Sun

perishes fast –
oh, everything but memory does not last!

Does it not last,
we all born from crematory ashes of our brothers
And sisters,
this sharpened, dominant cemetery!
Old flames, and smooth paper present,
burns to ashes our bones.
Let us collapse, devoid of spine, in anguish!
The cemetery, of sharpest memory, has us within
its immortal claws, again!

Religion's Cross

Man walks up to the cross,
knelt down on dry mud's tight-lipped mouth,
he knelt from suppleness through to frost,
with his head hung down South.

The histories bestowed for the believer,
the believer of whom wishes for re-enactment
to resurrect the game between a giver and receiver,
to silently beckon a gathering of a divine sacrament.

Man walks up to the cross,
offloaded his own silent cross of which thundered
to the ground incredibly,
and oh so indelibly branded in the pyre of the mind,
Oh, we die frequently, fall so heavily inside mentality
when we refuse for any reason not to collect God's
Gift from the cross,
like we refuse to drop to our knees and plead
for life's simple pleasures.
Man does not warm to humiliation nor treasure
the refusal another man makes in return...
but a cross to the ground, made to astound
our belief, to restore it, and the Stations of the Cross
are along with the cross of our very own – burnt...

Isn't it a form of tragedy?
Isn't it a form of travesty?
Isn't it a Sin of jealousy?
When Man watches another Man
Of whom is more than prepared to make that journey
that they struggled, more so could not achieve...
The cross of their own – remaining so heavily upon
nerves,

and a delay has potential to reap a man of years...

Maybe the man did kneel in front of the cross,
albeit maybe it was his own,
unknowingly peered into future,
I must disclose...
There existed no gathering,
he never stood on his soles again...

History was once penned,
but in one man's life...

Never again.

Statues of Rust

I wear the touch of your fingertips
upon my shoulders,
replacing wings that were torn
by the men; they hinder open lips
almost making the angel pole dance
inside of the borrowed hissing of flames,
before I wrapped one leg around his
coldest skin of heavy lust...
Heaven sent will to retaliate, and so
I returned back my barren land soaked in rain,
and every statue of him devalued in rust,
but in the fresh, young plain, starving
like deep lovers fading out of touch.
Foreign statues are less than bargain,
trespassing the distance for friendship
not sterling, just starting
my passion for love...

Your fingers curl tightly like rough
tides freeing themselves from their brothers,
richest anxiety shaking my passions
to my left foot and right foot of a resurrected
barren land travelled well when I had had enough
The businessmen hiding their breaking branches of points
behind their sauntering, feigning barks like lovers...
Like lovers pouring into my new land like red wine
into the picture; white walls – they may be transparency,
I don't fully lean on my mind as I do my heart's emotional beat,
behind the bare desolation of my land,
contrived, my share of salvation – hardly a natural hand

in the supple, cool earth.
But for love, I claim unnatural benefit of his concern, his care,
and whereof translation of his beautiful smile –
broken English doth speak: "You are hormonally mine,
and his loveable, sewn shirt; he, in dignified manner of sorts,
maintained a dormant, old heart; biblically lands cavorts, of great heights,
for miracles of Christ defied odds greater than the miracles themselves –
I do believe the miracle is I, but he is labelled with the price: "EQUALITY",
for he is my reflection of a dream, ice – he is upon it, conjured up from other men,
I pivot, nowhere I am to go, but falling on what I cannot show stamina upon.
And I am in his sight for many occasions, least when I am in flesh,
I am best a pavement to shake his stroll across the road of all his loves,
a road of which has no caution; to steal him from the lease of personal freedom.
I am steering him into the greatest of all realities, and he is my fortune,
for wherever he may seek his convenience, I am earned through his heart,
his passion to aid, his abolishment of misconduct on my behalf,
he recognises my character; at heart I am good,
for all of my endeavours to kill my passion to love –
the sanest of all faculties: our plutonic love.
The miracle of he and I, realists to the core,
exerting the ground built above all damnation we suffered hard –
We carry authority, possessing higher powers of Love,

leave, I turn to marry the open air -

Harshest consequence from making way down the sloping stair,
I made way, sought a face – he was there!

Because, because, perennially a statue in my land born of pain,
seen a horse, seen a horse, with mane of black,
some entity, some entity.
Some man, hath no label: "OBJECT" –
some man only wears material – is not material –
a ebony key strewn to piano – does not succumb into rust –
makes sweet music for eternity when not tampered with heavy tips of fingers,
few and far between; every white key bold white in satire, satirical on me –
burnt the candle- wick tether of me – stood in lieu dripping wax...

Latent Lover, a fine crush, a young flower, a borrowed brother,
his statue is growing! His muscle of heart untangled!
My heart in fatal asphyxiation, from the perimeter of heart around mine
like a belt around my waist!
Murdered my fiddled, played heart!
Stood in lieu a brand new harp!
His presence, vibration, my trembling world!
I risk for treasures and its perimeter of pleasures,
for each endeavour to seize him within my snare of patience,
patience as the night so dark with morbidity non-flight...

Well, I stand in my land of latent Love...
Stand so predictably beneath the subtle, shuffling breadth of cirrus,
Stand with shapeless shoulders, shapeless hands, shapeless face –
face hung into the surface - it shuffles in mind,
hands hung in suspense – they shuffle without clarity to stroke the air,
shoulders hung back in dislocation – they shuffle further behind...

No rain!
And he walked stiffly to face me...
Domineering, commanding, as the prey destined to die, one face suffice for my Love,
baptism of his dry hand healing and cleaning the furrowed brow,
inducted into his heart, as it knotted into a muscle once again,
and how quickly...

How quickly the rain fell...
He did not rust at all.

Stanzas (Written to the night)

I raised my chin profusely,
when night was silently dead,
Toward the upper atmosphere,
where dark and light were paired.
As moon had cast a sphere,
it's glowing, hazy circumference,
I watched from afar with gravity,
as it lost the fullest of clarities.

The moon made an appearance,
to sleep above public watch,
And scattered randomly and sparsely,
were illuminated, shying dots,
Awaiting the performing starlings,
by which time, the dots - no more,
And I watched from afar with fear,
as spread-winged owls began to cheer!

The trees began to sway,
complimentary to the winds of plangent,
From afar, the reprised wolf,
it's deep cries signalling the danger,
In other than the rough of the bull,
but of the hills that do bear eyes,
And as I watched from afar with fright,
two eyes did emerge from the night!

As madness of the time crept upon me,
I felt my pulse like no other,
Racing toward some attack,
with this heart inside of another.
My sight became of that outside some Cadillac,
peering through tinted windows without success,

Now this horrid phantasmagoria,
of such deep, unsettling aura!
Maybe the time will confirm one's fear,
that the night is here to stay,
And of all that I hold so dear,
will become stranded in the fearless day!

Tears In Their City

My heart's desire runs
through the maelstrom of
held hands and the passing
city of lovesick souls,
inside this city of embraces
and strengths.
The souls of Love are
travelling distant lengths,
the cold metal claws are
nightly holding intense heat
That they were created
to hold,
so much a city,
and I do not live it,
sat lonesome in the metal
heights,
holding the city in my
tear-laden eye,
an eye kept warm, releases
tears, given it
doth not make the city of
Love,
the deserted land of a
thousand struggling smiles,
otherwise, I would with born
dry face,
be gloating,
bemoaning,
down upon the city from my
fantastic unreality of space.

Starvation Lands: Waiting on the Captain

Marooned upon the starvation sands,
hallowed be the flag,
hallowed be the captain.
The time roughly drags
in flush to reach the place
where sea and land link
and banish, make good
fill of the space,
link like doomed newlyweds,
unknowingly tied for a lifetime
in pretty, strong lace.
Endurable,
living upon starvation lands,
Endurable –
it is the only way,
Endurable,
and the man devoid of religion heart
has for days, issued forth the word of God;
He prays,
plays the game of faith,
whether or not he truly believes,
he is waiting on the captain.

But the torn halyard broke,
torn again, but for the final time
and his suffering skin is all
wrapped in
thick sadism of the air that
stood still,
will and forever more;
through all seasons and never

had one saw
such wane in comparison to all men,
will and forever more…
We will see his eyes again,
even they do not bring forth
the seas,
this land is water-less,
to morph; the metamorphosis,
power to bring ten thousand men
to their living peril
and bring out of a man
all seven
deadliest sins a Devil made!

*The captain has retreated
to the lighthouse,
That falsest of marooned Man's
hopes,
This heart-breaking of all
facades!*

The Road Taken

Two roads posed in front of
my view,
like ourselves in passport
booths.
And if only then I knew,
from belated, sinister proof,
the saddening, harrowing truth,
that evil mind doth do,
to my fearless, stubborn soul,
its potential to shift and move
volently the courageous heart,
to reduce one's courage to start,
to a cowering, lonely creature,
and of which one's paper is
permanently marked,
with inerasable misery.
Because one of two roads I
chose,
I thought so naively there was no
difference
and I did not ponder to pose,
that life-deciding significance,
to why one road; to Hell it goes,
and would beg of me deliverance
and I in turn will beg,
for the walk to be reversed.
But that this responsibility shared,
is made for us damned and cursed
and that into harmful, troubling waters,
so hot, we will surely burn
and become at one with waters'
drowning, bad inferno,
of which we won't return,

and this road; made to make
these journeys unto damned,
and thus; remnants of goodness I
must forsake,
on the road leading to unspeakable
lands.
The other road was not meant
for me and my foot that make print
and this place by foot I was sent,
I have not seen footprints since,
the place where time is drunk,
where disorderly pendulums are,
where one's heart is permanently shrunk,
and one's humour in a jar,
pendulums regularly shatter
like gunshots in the trenches
and I cannot escape this personified
fear.
I am in a losing battle
and now such difference is crystalline
clear.

The Waiting Room

The queue at the door of Death
stretches like a desperate arm,
And there is no breath,
no creases upon the many palms.

Door caparisoned with sugar paper,
black, with childish stuck-on stars,
To walk through this door – this is safer,
than another door, branded "the dark"…

Through the door, one by one,
follow in the footsteps of ones
dead in different ways; door to a room that held the Sun,
whilst inside the other room, held a sun that runs,
captured, agonizing purgatory.

Relive oblivion with a sigh of relief,
maybe a third time to be completely honest…
That they honestly absorbed the Sun's rays and donned the golden wreath,
if prematurely inducted into the Sun, the room would be certain to grow pain that they inherit…
Regardless of whether they truly want it.

A childish door to show they never lost themselves,
to show they never lost a childhood, just left it.
But the other door is without such child's contribution,
the bells that signal entry sound like a demon's
alluring, deceiving flute that carries the tune in an air of deficit…

The queue never loses such great a stretch as this,

the outstretched arm of Man opens the door,
They say it's the arm of Christ,
How many more?
Once, they lost sight of Christ,
wrapped in the playful blanket of childishness,
But before the door, they look that someone in the eye,
maybe that someone died,
maybe he was the first,
and maybe the dead are still learning...

To Cherish, My Dear

I cannot admire the conceited
all my youthful days,
I cherish the king's men
before the king, any day,
because the likeliness of my defeat is
that likeliness of kings' vainglory,
when he cheats a place of hearts:
my weapons are becoming poorly.

But cherish you, your king's loud hubris-
your quiet pride,
I cherish you madly as a thorn
taken out, and on the floor by my side.
Your eyes make my slippery, unblemished face,
I never looked in an eye so lubricous,
cruel to be kind in the wounded place.
I cherish you, dear,
clenched fist in pride,
to know you dear,
my thorn in my side - you took it from me,
dear
and replaced my lazily, hung red hood
with a clean veil of a bride.
I cherish you, dear,
wet, modest miracles hung out to dry,
I cherish you out of fear,
but in fickle fantasies, I cannot say goodbye.

The Wooded Landscape

Barks climb through the sky,
or so it looks from a distance
and a lake reflects a rude awakening;
the ground lays dead and dried.

I see through one's eager eye
a debris of woodland murder,
I see it through one's inquisitive look –
the disease out of barks' contagious burdens.

Lend my shoulders to carry the dead
and why –
when it looks not part of I from distance,
when the lake reflects woodland's
spirit in pressing state.
I do not want stain upon my
existence!

Barks climb to the filthy lake,
or so it looks from distance;
my despair – the rude awakening,
is exposed through
despair of landscape
I trace…
In melancholia of states...

Vantage Point

I stood on some small hill,
and I had everything in view
and the lament of a midnight chill,
made constant talk in the air of June.

With some amulet I wore,
to bade farewell to the Devil,
the evil that I saw,
was all about my level.

Ornate in Catholic values,
I began to proffer some moon
with faith,
for he is only silver,
and for belief, he came too late.

Imbue him with copper and gold,
and hone his secret eye,
so that then he will behold,
some religion before he dies.

Up in a midnight sky,
where all ilk of creation doth lie,
the sun and moon; at separation they live,
but then... they always die.

To You (Mother)

Roses are complicated,
but intensely passionate,
Violets are our skies at dusk,
but as much as a gyration of seas,
And although the orris-iris brings
about our necks the scent of musk,
You mean as much to me,
and if anything – more,
Than what these rooted creatures
could drop and pour,
And bow at my feet,
through Summer evenings,
Or as I gaze supinely as they
spritely soar,
Making of me much less
or something more,
But you,
you bore me into this world,
Inside of you,
Months spent tightly curled,
inside of the womb,
But you,
who makes that sadness blue,
For you add to a great sorrow,
a lighter hue,
But you, you
make that beauty truth,
But you, you
who gave me life, and then
Spurned me to write this
with eager pen,
And a loving heart...
I love you,

and my love for you
Is no dying art,
as timeless as glass,
Well so are you,
and, I love you.

Vitula Sweet Music

Pulsating rhythm of sweet
vitula,
guttural trills,
forcing one's soul in one's
feet,
one's body complete,
a sentimental mover.
Over the hills,
I heard a sound no truer
than that of sweet Vitula.

Harmonious drones; horse
hair of bow,
swirling notes,
stirring one's soul
in rose red nutmeg,
making of one as whole,
as whole as one can get.
My soul furrowed,
with Vitula's coarse coats,
My heart; a filled burrow,
by the rush of horse hair bow.

My sweet Vitula, sweet music,
soothe my soul
and caress my heart,
with a timeless art,
as that of sweet Vitula,
a sentimental mover,
moved me while I sat,
pounced upon my shell
like a cat,
took me by one foot,

and then by the other,
stepping fervently,
thy enlightened brother.
There is a hill that converges
with the stream,
Let thy stream of thy conscience
make thy dream,
And if a dream is but that,
and nothing more,
Let me indulge in passion's
desire,
And let my sweet Vitula take
thy soul; take mine essence,
And sprinkle it upon a
paradise.
And make of me renaissance
from thy dreams,
make one feel reborn
from music's realm
and make one's conscience
consistently free,
with sweet Vitula,
soul's sentimental mover!
I am one with the strings,
I confess I am redeemed,
those beautiful things,
dressed in coffee coats,
the magic one hears,
of those pitching notes,
My sweet Vitula,
music to one's cold old ears.

We Call Them Roses

Fine, ready growths,
we call them roses,
dressed in seraphic coats,
the coats of scarlet it
poaches.
From the blushing of cheeks,
of two sweethearts standing,
eyes, averted to the roses,
while hearts of both demanding,
The lovely scent of rose,
be scattered on their pillows
and everywhere their feet go,
amongst the stealthy willows,
in the distance far,
throughout the growing
seasons.
Below the midnight lark,
the roses, some of which,
Through every season,
bloom,
Through winter, they will stitch,
the fellow flowers' wounds,
who mourn the loss of climbing,
progression is the heights,
but in winter, they are dying,
perishing, stagnant,
in our sights.

Hybrid tears a plenty,
the colour and size of Hybrid,
the lengthy blooming,
sent Tea,
throughout the season,

long,
the vigorous growth
that time bred,
that progresses in a romantic
song.
The rose,
our love,
our symbol,
our life of love
that's nimble.

www.ingramcontent.com/pod-product-compliance
Lightning Source LLC
Chambersburg PA
CBHW022119090426
42743CB00008B/917